FOOD SUPPLY

Andrew J. Milson, Ph.D.
Content Consultant
University of Texas at Arlington

Acknowledgments

Grateful acknowledgment is given to the authors, artists, photographers, museums, publishers, and agents for permission to reprint copyrighted material. Every effort has been made to secure the appropriate permission. If any omissions have been made or if corrections are required, please contact the Publisher.

Instructional Consultant: Christopher Johnson, Evanston, Illinois

Teacher Reviewers: Leah Perry, Exploris Middle School, Raleigh, North Carolina
Erin Stevens, Quabbin Regional Middle/High School, Barre, Massachusetts

Text Credits

11 Excerpt from "Bangladesh: Thousands flee Floods," August 22, 2011, by IRIN. Copyright © by IRIN. Reprinted by permission of IRINnews.org.

Photographic Credits

Cover, Inside Front Cover, Title Page ©Keren Su/Corbis. **3** (bg) ©David Toase/Stockbyte/Getty Images. **4** (bg) ©Steve Winter/National Geographic Stock. **6** (bg) ©REUTERS/Finbarr O'Reilly. **7** (tl) ©Jake Lyell/Alamy. **8** (bg) Mapping Specialists. **10** (bg) ©Jorgen Schytte/Still Pictures/Aurora Photos.
13 (bg) ©REUTERS/Rafiqur Rahman.
14 (t) ©David Woodfall/StillPictures/Aurora Photos. (cr) ©David Woodfall/StillPictures/Aurora Photos. **16** (bg) ©REUTERS/Luc Gnago. **17** (tl) ©James L. Stanfield/National Geographic Stock.
19 (bg) ©REUTERS/Luc Gnago. **20** (t) ©REUTERS/Luc Gnago. **22** (bg) ©Marshall Burke. **23** (tl) ©Zacharie Sero Tamou. **24** (cr) ©Lennart Woltering.
25 (bg) ©Joerg Boethling/Alamy. **27** (t) ©Gage/Getty Images. **28** (tr) ©Gary K Smith/Garden Picture Library/Getty Images. **30** (br) ©Jake Lyell/Alamy. (tr) ©Janet Jarman/Corbis News/Corbis.
31 (bg) ©David Toase/Stockbyte/Getty Images. (bl) ©James L. Stanfield/National Geographic Stock. (tr) ©James P. Blair/National Geographic Stock. (br) ©REUTERS/Stringer.

MetaMetrics® and the MetaMetrics logo and tagline are trademarks of MetaMetrics, Inc., and are registered in the United States and abroad. The trademarks and names of other companies and products mentioned herein are the property of their respective owners. Copyright © 2010 MetaMetrics, Inc. All rights reserved.

Visit National Geographic Learning online at www.NGSP.com.

Visit our corporate website at www.cengage.com.

Printed in the USA.

RR Donnelley, Menasha, WI

ISBN: 978-07362-97578

14 15 16 17 18 19 20 21 22

10 9 8 7 6 5 4 3 2

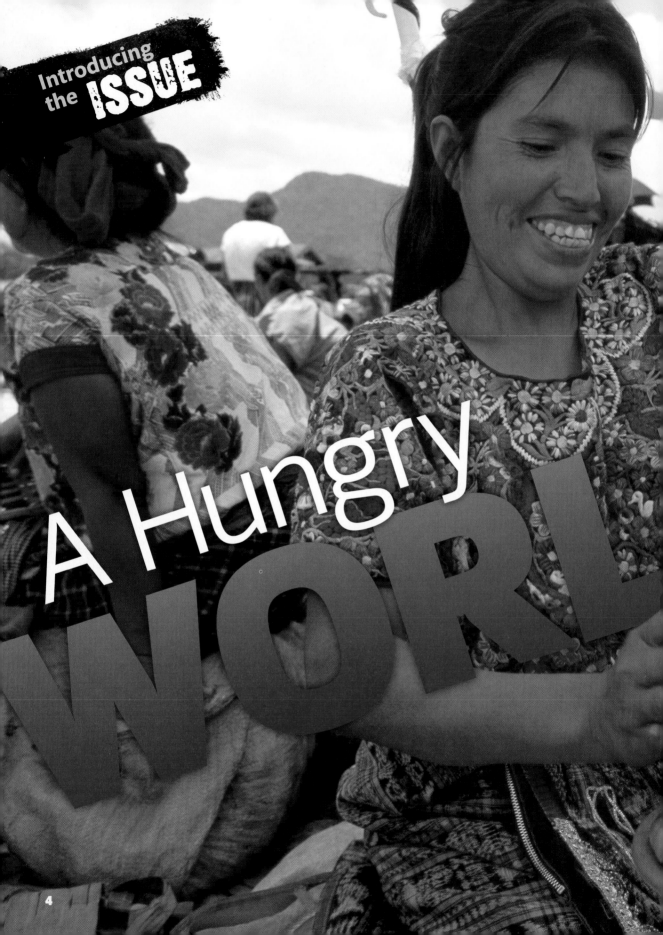

A Hungry WORLD

HOW DO YOU FEED 7 BILLION PEOPLE?

Since there is sufficient food in the world for everyone, no one has to worry about having enough to eat, right? If you agreed with that statement, you would be wrong! The world has 7 billion people, of whom nearly 1 billion go hungry every day. In fact, there are more hungry people in the world than the populations of the United States, Canada, and the European Union combined. As the planet's population increases, the number of people without access to adequate food will increase as well.

A woman sells produce at a market in Guatemala. Much of the world's food is grown by small farmers and sold at markets such as this one.

FOOD IS LIFE

For thousands of years, people all over the world have practiced **agriculture**, the raising of food. Agriculture, or farming, includes working the soil to grow crops such as corn, beans, or melons; raising animals for meat or milk; and planting trees that produce fruit, nuts, coffee beans, or tea leaves.

Without the nourishment and energy you receive from food, survival would be impossible. Nutritious food in sufficient quantities is essential for good health. Yet many people cannot afford to purchase enough food for themselves and their families, or they lack land on which to grow the food they need to nourish themselves.

More than a thousand women and children wait in line for emergency food aid in a village in Niger, in western Africa. Several international organizations exist to provide food to people who suffer from hunger caused by drought or other natural disasters.

Children receive food aid in Malawi, southern Africa.

EMPTY FOOD BOWLS

Even people who have the skills to cultivate their own food can be at risk of starvation. Small farmers are often poor, and when their crops fail or sell at low prices, they go hungry.

Sometimes food in a region becomes extremely scarce, and this scarcity, or **famine**, can lead to starvation and even death. When crops that are an area's major food source fail, famine becomes a serious menace. Crops can fail for a number of reasons, including depleted soil and **drought**—an extended period without rain. Plant diseases, insects, extreme weather, and war can also destroy crops and create famine.

Some people with low incomes live in **food deserts**, areas where stores that sell nutritious foods are too far away to reach easily. A food desert can be in the middle of a bustling city or out in the country. Even in times of plenty for everyone else, people living in a food desert are at risk of going hungry or suffering from illnesses because the only food that is easily available is not healthful.

WHERE'S DINNER?

Making sure the world's people have adequate food involves new ways of thinking about food supply. In urban areas, for example, people have begun growing food in their yards and even on their roofs. In remote rural areas, people are striving to increase food yields by making the most of the available soil and water resources.

In the following pages you will read about how people in Bangladesh and West Africa are coping with issues involving **food security**—regular, sustained access to sufficient and nutritious food.

Explore the Issue

1. **Identify** Why is agriculture necessary to people?

2. **Analyze Cause and Effect** Name two or three reasons why 1 billion people do not have enough food.

Hunger in Our

Undernourished people of the world by percentage of total population

- more than or equal to 35%
- 20–34%
- 10–19%
- 5–9%
- less than 5%
- Incomplete data

N O R T H
A M E R I C A

NORTH
ATLANTIC
OCEAN

UNITED STATES An estimated 13.5 million Americans—most of whom have low incomes—live in food deserts, where sources of nutritious food are distant or difficult to reach.

HAITI Haiti is one of the world's poorest countries, and about one-third of Haiti's people suffer from food insecurity, or lack of access to sufficient nutritious food.

CASE STUDY 2

WEST AFRICA
Millions of farmers in West Africa struggle to feed their families. Côte d'Ivoire, the world's leading producer of cocoa, has one of the world's highest poverty rates.

BOLIVIA In Bolivia, one of the poorest countries in Latin America, two-thirds of the people live below the poverty line. Many cannot afford to purchase adequate food.

S O U T H
A M E R I C A

SOUTH
PACIFIC
OCEAN

SOUTH
ATLANTIC
OCEAN

Explore the Issue

1. **Interpret Maps** Which continent has the largest number of countries colored in red? What does this mean?

2. **Draw Conclusions** Is agriculture successful in addressing hunger in West Africa? Why or why not?

World

Study the map below to learn about the nearly 1 billion people throughout the world who are suffering from hunger.

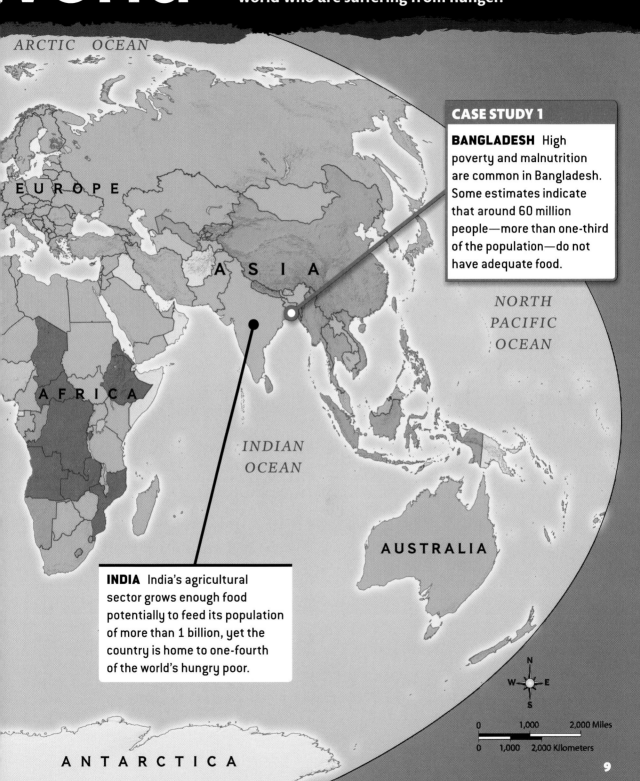

ARCTIC OCEAN

EUROPE

ASIA

AFRICA

NORTH PACIFIC OCEAN

INDIAN OCEAN

AUSTRALIA

ANTARCTICA

CASE STUDY 1

BANGLADESH High poverty and malnutrition are common in Bangladesh. Some estimates indicate that around 60 million people—more than one-third of the population—do not have adequate food.

INDIA India's agricultural sector grows enough food potentially to feed its population of more than 1 billion, yet the country is home to one-fourth of the world's hungry poor.

N
W   E
S

0   1,000   2,000 Miles

0   1,000   2,000 Kilometers

A man transports rice, one of Bangladesh's main crops. The country's rice crop has doubled since 1970.

Feeding the HUNGRY in Bangladesh

DEVASTATED BY FLOODS

Bangladesh (ban-gluh-DESH) is a South Asian country with high levels of poverty and food insecurity. The country also suffers the effects of nature's forces at their most destructive.

In the summer of 2011, storms and floods affected more than 1.5 million people in Bangladesh. Forced to leave their homes, many had no alternative but to construct temporary shelters along the roadsides. Across the country, people urgently needed food, water, and shelter. One woman lamented, "The flood has washed away all our happiness. My son had three acres of . . . rice crops and all is now underwater. What will we eat now? My family will starve."

The disaster would not end with the receding of the floodwaters. One official with an aid organization predicted continuing troubles. "When the flood water goes down," he claimed, "dead plants, livestock and other perishables will start to rot and provide a thriving breeding ground for microbes responsible for water-borne diseases. That is the biggest health risk associated with flood."

LABORATORY FOR DISASTER

Crises of this magnitude have been all too common in the history of Bangladesh. In recent decades, the country has suffered numerous disasters, including droughts, storm surges, cyclones, and chronic flooding.

Because Bangladesh is a low-lying country, it is particularly threatened by rising sea levels, an effect of **climate change**, the gradual warming of Earth's temperatures. Estimates vary, but scientists predict the seas may rise by 3 feet or more during this century alone, which would flood large areas of the country. According to different calculations, a rise of 3 feet could affect between 15 million and 30 million people. In one of the world's most densely populated countries, relocation would be extremely difficult, if not impossible, and mass **migrations**, movements of people from one country or area to another, would occur.

The combined and growing threats from nature have led one observer to describe Bangladesh as "nature's laboratory on natural disaster."

WATER EVERYWHERE

Bangladesh is located at the delta of three major river systems that empty into the Bay of Bengal. With climate change causing heavier monsoons (mahn-SOONZ), river flooding has increased.

Monsoons are seasonal changes in the direction of the prevailing winds. In Bangladesh, farmers would normally welcome the heavy rains that the summer monsoons bring. The more intense monsoons of recent years, however, have been overwhelming. In some areas, the land has become too **saturated**, or filled with water, to absorb more water. As a result, the water pools on top of the land.

In August of 2011, the homes and farms of an estimated 57,000 people had been flooded and were likely to remain submerged for weeks. In one waterlogged region in the south, poor farmers suffered severe losses when flooding damaged or destroyed 66,000 acres of crops.

A SINKING LAND

Water is at the heart of other challenges facing Bangladesh's farmers. As the climate has heated up, rain patterns have changed. Water that floods the land often deposits salt, which makes soil infertile.

Some efforts to control flooding have backfired. In the 1960s, for example, aid organizations tried to protect rice farmers from flooding by building **dikes**, banks of earth that control the flow of water. Before the dikes were built, rivers had overflowed onto fields and then receded, depositing sediment that built up the land. Without regular flooding from the rivers, the fields no longer received fresh layers of sediment. In addition, the soil was compacted, or tightly packed, which caused the land to sink.

The sinking land created serious consequences for Bangladesh's rice farmers. Rice plants need a wet environment, so rice farmers kept their fields, also called paddies, flooded much of the time. Still, it is sometimes necessary to drain the paddies. When rice fields sank below river level, water in the paddies could no longer drain away, causing the fields to become unproductive.

These women in Bangladesh are collecting spinach leaves from a flooded field in 2004. The flood put almost 3 million acres of land under water.

UNDOING THE DAMAGE

In the face of these challenges, Bangladeshi farmers have sought their own solutions. In 1997, a group of farmers cut through a dike so that sediment-filled water could flow onto their fields. Three years later, sediment had built up the land by about four feet. Cutting through dikes also allowed water to drain off fields that had been submerged by flooding. Observing these results, the government began encouraging people to use water flow to manage sediment.

One organization is encouraging Bangladeshis to raise crabs as well as shrimp in the delta of the Ganges River. Raising only one species could be harmful to the river's environment.

To overcome the problem of **brackish**, or salty, water, Bangladeshis have developed salt-resistant strains of rice. As a result, the country's production of rice, its most important product, has doubled since the early 1970s.

In the south, where flooding has turned fields into brackish ponds, farmers have adapted by raising saltwater species such as shrimp and crabs.

Children fish for shrimp fry, or immature shrimp, in an area that has suffered damage by a typhoon.

A RESILIENT PEOPLE

The people of Bangladesh cope with floods in a variety of ways. Some dismantle their flooded homes and move to higher ground, while others create floating gardens on which to plant food crops. Floating hospitals and libraries operate in flooded areas, and children attend floating schools. People who live on *chars*, small islands in the floodplains of Bangladesh's rivers, move from one *char* to another as the rivers' flow and tides cause the islands to rise and fall.

In the face of many obstacles, the people of Bangladesh have learned that innovation and adaptation are the keys to raising food on their constantly changing land.

Explore the Issue

1. **Summarize** How have the people of Bangladesh adapted to increased flooding?

2. **Analyze Causes and Effects** How has flooding affected agriculture in Bangladesh?

HUNGER
IN CÔTE D'IVOIR'

Making chocolate from cocoa beans is a long process. Before they are shipped to chocolate factories in other countries, the beans are fermented and then laid out to dry. In this photo, farmers gather the dried cocoa beans.

A REGION OF CONTRASTS

West Africa is a region of contrasts, and Côte d'Ivoire (KOHT dee-VWAHR) is a prime example. Despite being the world's leading producer of **cocoa**, the main ingredient of chocolate, Côte d'Ivoire is one of the world's 20 poorest countries. The country enjoyed relative stability and prosperity in the 1990s, but since then it has experienced political and military conflicts, causing massive population displacement and increased food insecurity. Environmental problems also threaten the food supply in Côte d'Ivoire.

A newly harvested pod reveals fresh cocoa beans.

Small-scale farmers make up most of the poor in Côte d'Ivoire. In the northern part of the country, farmers struggle to raise grains, cotton, and livestock. Intensive farming has used up the nutrients in the soil, leading to soil infertility, and climate change has affected rainfall patterns.

Another problem is that, unlike fruits and vegetables, cocoa is not a crop farmers can use to feed themselves and their families. Cocoa beans are not edible until they have been processed. In the forest areas of southern Côte d'Ivoire, farmers grow cocoa for cash, but if the crop does not sell for a high enough price, farmers may not have enough money to purchase food for their families.

REAPING COCOA, NOT PROFIT

Although the global chocolate industry is worth billions of dollars, cocoa growers in West Africa receive only a small share of the profits. Côte d'Ivoire and its neighbor Ghana (GAH-nuh) produce more than 50 percent of the world's cocoa, yet in Côte d'Ivoire 40 percent of the population lives below the poverty line. In Ghana, household income for cocoa growers is just a few dollars per day.

Ninety percent of Africa's cocoa is grown on small family farms, most of which have only 2 hectares (about 5 acres) or less of land. These small spaces limit the amount of cocoa a farmer can produce. In addition, years of failure to enrich the soil have led to poor soil quality and decreasing yields.

1.8 MILLION CHILD LABORERS

Many poor small farmers cannot afford to educate their children, nor can they afford to hire farm labor. Instead, they put their children to work in the cocoa fields. Children perform many light tasks but also some that are dangerous. For example, injuries are frequent among children wielding large, sharp knives to break open cocoa pods. Exposure to pesticides also puts children at risk.

Sometimes children are sent to other farms, or even sold as slaves. Estimates of enslaved children on cocoa farms range from 12,000 to 15,000. However, a recent report indicated that more than 1.8 million children in West Africa, whether slaves or workers on their family's farms, were involved in growing cocoa.

KNOWLEDGE IS THE KEY

To generate an adequate living from their small farms, cocoa farmers must make the most of their limited resources. Unfortunately, many are unaware of how to increase yields or combat diseases that attack their crops.

Farmers in Côte d'Ivoire, for example, mistakenly tied plastic strips around their trees to deter the onset of "black pod," a fungus that destroys cocoa pods. In an effort to improve soil fertility, farmers also spread blackened pods around the base of cocoa trees, which actually spread the disease.

Said one frustrated farmer after learning the cause of black pod, "Ignorance is the base of the misfortunes of many cocoa farmers in Côte d'Ivoire."

Some organizations have been helping cocoa farmers educate themselves. The World Cocoa Foundation (WCF), for example, trains farmers to improve quality and efficiency, **diversification** (raising more than one crop), and business skills.

Farmer Marc Guré shows how effective the WCF's approach can be. Along with cocoa, Guré began raising pineapple, papaya, and yams to sell at a local market. He uses **sustainable**—or environmentally responsible—practices by making use of everything he can. Instead of discarding cocoa pod husks, he burns them. Then his wife uses the ash to make soap. Guré's small farm is one of the most profitable in his area.

A young boy gathers cocoa pods in a field in Niable, Ivory Coast.

WOMEN MAKE THE DIFFERENCE

Women are an integral part of the labor force on cocoa farms. Yet when the World Cocoa Foundation began training farmers in West Africa, female involvement was low. Many women were too busy raising children, hauling water, gathering fuel, and working in the fields to participate. To increase women's access to training, WCF developed Video Viewing Clubs so that women could view training videos at their convenience.

Another WCF program, Empowering Cocoa Households, or ECHOES, seeks to create a better livelihood for the next generation. ECHOES offers scholarships for children's school expenses alongside business training for mothers. Women gain the skills they need to generate more income, and increased profits pay for their children's education. With a better education, the children of cocoa farmers will have greater access to jobs beyond the hard work of harvesting and processing cocoa. Some may even return to the cocoa plantations with new ideas for improving farmers' lives.

Rows of cocoa plants grow abundantly on a farm in Bonoua in eastern Côte d'Ivoire.

PATHS TO FOOD SECURITY

Other organizations are approaching the problems of small cocoa farmers from a different angle. They encourage companies that make and sell chocolate to engage in **fair trade**, paying farmers fair prices and investing in cocoa-producing communities. Fair trade allows cocoa growers to keep a larger amount of the profit from their labor.

Improving the livelihood of struggling cocoa farmers is no small task. Nevertheless, fair prices, training, and more productive growing practices are slowly helping to improve food security for an increasing number of cocoa farmers.

Explore the Issue

1. **Analyze Causes** Why are West African cocoa growers poor?
2. **Identify Problems and Solutions** How are cocoa growers increasing their food security?

A "Green" Approach to Relieving Hunger

A woman harvests lettuce during the dry season in Dunkassa, Benin. Solar powered drip irrigation has allowed people to grow nutritious vegetables during the long 8-month dry season.

FAR FROM SIMPLE

Environmental scientist Jennifer Burney is concerned that solutions to world hunger may contribute to a different problem—climate change. In turn, climate change adds complexity to the challenge of defeating hunger.

Growing food can create pollution. Runoff water from irrigation may wash chemical fertilizers and pesticides into lakes and streams. Tractors and other fuel-driven farm equipment produce greenhouse gases that contribute to global warming.

As Earth warms, weather patterns become more irregular, making crops harder to grow. More frequent hurricanes and other forms of extreme weather cause intense rains, which cause flooding.

Jennifer Burney works with villagers in Africa.

Progress and growth in agriculture can bring great benefits, creating a more plentiful and varied food supply. Yet the consequences of that progress, as you have just learned, can be harmful. As a National Geographic Emerging Explorer, Jennifer Burney is working with the Society to find a balance. She is striving to reduce hunger while protecting the environment. In sub-Saharan Africa, she works with poor farmers struggling to raise food. "We are a world of plenty, yet almost a billion people don't have enough to eat," notes Burney.

HARNESSING THE SUN

At a test site in Benin (BEH-nin) in West Africa, Burney has tapped into the sun's energy to power irrigation systems. With support from the Solar Electric Light Fund, she has helped set up solar-powered water pumps that regulate the amount of water the irrigation systems receive. On sunny days the pumps work faster, and on cloudy days they work slower. This ensures that the crops, which need more water on sunny days, get the amount of water they need. Since no fuel is burned to produce power, no pollutants are released into the air.

Three years after its installation, the system has improved the farmers' lives. They are able to grow greater quantities of fruits and vegetables. Consequently, they have more money to buy food and to send their children to school.

CLEANER COOKING

According to Burney, reducing the harmful effects of cooking on the environment is also important. Cooking uses about 8 percent of global energies and is especially inefficient in developing nations. Stoves traditionally used in these countries burn wood or dung, which creates soot. When soot is released in homes, it can make people ill. Outside, the black particles can seriously harm the environment by speeding up the melting of glaciers, altering monsoon cycles, and contributing to global warming.

In India, Burney is working on a project to replace traditional cooking stoves with more efficient ones. Early results indicate that the eco-stoves release fewer emissions into the air and also require less fuel.

Jennifer Burney is convinced that replacing traditional stoves is the most effective way to immediately begin slowing climate change. She hopes that developing countries will do so, and soon.

MAKE A DIFFERENCE

As Burney notes, hunger will not be relieved through one grand, sweeping solution. In each part of the world, different factors contribute to hunger, and each solution must be weighed against possible consequences.

You can join in the search for solutions to hunger. First, learn all you can about how and where food is raised, nutrition, climate change, and other matters relating to hunger. Decisions made anywhere on Earth about food production and land use affect you, so understand what's happening.

You can also find ways to take action. The activity on the next two pages can help you be part of the solution to hunger in your own community.

Jennifer Burney and farmers in Bessassi, Benin, inspect the farmers' solar-powered water pumps.

Explore the Issue

1. **Analyze Causes** What is the relationship between agriculture and the environment?

2. **Identify Problems and Solutions** Why does Jennifer Burney believe that cooking with eco-stoves in developing nations can slow climate change?

"We are a world of plenty, yet almost a billion people don't have enough to eat." —Jennifer Burney

A woman in West Africa uses a solar cooker to prepare a meal. Unlike some traditional stoves, a solar cooker does not release harmful substances into the air.

Volunteer
at a Community
Garden
—and share your results

The solution to world hunger may begin at home. Get involved by volunteering at a community garden and raising fresh fruits and vegetables. The healthy food you grow will help feed hungry people in your part of the world.

IDENTIFY

- Research local community gardens that grow produce.

- Phone or visit the gardens you are interested in to find out about the different tasks you might be asked to do.

- Get the facts by asking how much food the garden typically produces each year and how the food is distributed to those who need it.

ORGANIZE

- Figure out how much time you can devote to the community garden each week and create a schedule.

- Gather whatever tools you'll need for your work in the garden, such as gloves, shovels, rakes, and trowels.

- Recruit friends and family members who are also willing to work in the community garden during the growing season.

A teacher and her students tend the garden they have planted at their school. These herbs and vegetables could help feed people in the community.

DOCUMENT

- Take before, during, and after photos of the community garden and videos of work sessions.

- Keep a record of what is planted in the community garden as well as yields for each type of herb, fruit, or vegetable.

- Jot down your experiences with the plants, the work, and your fellow volunteers and note what you learned in a journal.

SHARE

- Use your photos and videos to create a multimedia presentation of the community garden project and show it to your class.

- Propose that your school start a community garden project that students can help organize and run.

- Write a feature article for your local paper describing your volunteer work and how it made a difference to you and your community.

Write a How-To Guide

You have volunteered at a community garden in which you helped grow food. Draw on that experience and do some further research to write a how-to guide for others who wish to plant a garden. A clear, well-written gardening guide may inspire friends and family members to start growing food themselves.

RESEARCH

Use the Internet, books, and articles as well as your own experiences in a community garden to research and answer the following questions:

- What soil and sun conditions are best for growing produce in your community?
- When is the best planting time for these food crops?
- How much water and fertilizer do the plants require?

As you do your research, be sure to take notes. Check your sources for accuracy and credibility.

DRAFT

Review your notes and then write a first draft.

- Introduce your topic clearly, previewing what is to follow in your how-to guide.
- Use bullet points to list the steps in the gardening process. Develop the steps using relevant facts and concrete details from your experience in the garden.
- Use appropriate transitions to clarify the relationships among your ideas and the steps in the process.
- Inform your readers using precise language and vocabulary that is specific to gardening.
- In the last paragraph, provide a concluding statement that follows from and supports the information you presented in your introduction and step-by-step list.

REVISE & EDIT

Read your first draft to make sure that it provides step-by-step information on starting a garden.

- Do you clearly introduce the topic of your how-to guide?
- Do the steps contain helpful, relevant, and concrete information?
- Are the transitions between the steps clear and easy to follow?
- Do you use precise, gardening-specific language?
- Does your conclusion sum up and support the information and explanations in your guide?

Revise the how-to guide to make sure you have covered all the bases. Then check your paper for errors in spelling and punctuation.

PUBLISH & PRESENT

Now you are ready to publish and present your how-to guide. Add any images that may help explain the steps you describe. Then print out your guide or write a clean copy by hand. Consider placing the guide in your school library for others to use.

Visual GLOSSARY

agriculture

food security

agriculture *n.*, the raising of food

brackish *adj.*, salty

climate change *n.*, gradual changes in Earth's temperatures

cocoa *n.*, the main ingredient of chocolate

dike *n.*, a bank of earth that is used to control the flow of of water over land

diversification *n.*, in agriculture, raising more than one crop

drought *n.*, a long period without rain

fair trade *n.*, a system that pays farmers a fair price for their produce

famine *n.*, an extreme scarcity of food

food desert *n.*, a place where there is no nearby source of healthful food

food security *n.*, regular access to adequate food

migration *n.*, the movement of people from one country or area to another

monsoon *n.*, seasonal change in prevailing winds that brings heavy rains

saturated *adj.*, containing the greatest amount of liquid that can be absorbed; unable to absorb more liquid

sustainable *adj.*, environmentally responsible; using resources wisely to avoid depleting them

monsoon

drought

cocoa

INDEX

SKILLS